DADTASTIC

WHY YOU'RE SO AMAZING

This edition published in 2022
By SJG Publishing, HP22 6NF, UK

Author: Helen Vaux
Cover design: Milestone Creative
Contents design: Seagulls

978-1-913004-38-5

Printed in China

10 9 8 7 6 5 4 3 2 1

Contents

Introduction

"Being a dad isn't just about eating a huge bag of gummy bears as your wife gives birth. It means being comfortable with the word 'hero'."

Ryan Reynolds

What is it that makes dads 'dadtastic'? Of course, it's not just one thing. The brilliance of dads is made up of a whole bundle of wonderful elements – even those that their children sometimes find exasperating! This book is here to tell dads about every last little thing that makes them a source of strength, love and laughs.

Every dad is different, but they all have something in common – their children. Sometimes, kids forget to tell their dads how they feel about them, not because they don't want to but because life – and embarrassment! – can simply get in the way. So, it's time to celebrate why dads mean everything to us and how they make the world a brighter place. Whether it's for their dancing skills, financial nous or their words of wisdom, never, ever underestimate a dad!

By the end of this book, dads will feel prouder than the day their children were born (well, almost!). Not only proud of themselves, but proud of the awesome humans they've helped create and nurture. And perhaps they will stop being so modest and finally say out loud: "I'm a dad and, yes, I'm dadtastic!"

Why Dads
ARE THE BEST

Dads are awesome. Trouble is, they don't get told enough! If you're a dad who's feeling a little unloved, read on. These are just some of the reasons why you're *numero uno*...

....

... You're always there with a hug, a nugget of wisdom and a joke when things are tough.

... You've not forgotten what it's like to be young.
(And can therefore forgive A LOT.)

... You can tolerate mess without ordering a
rapid response clean-up operation.

... Even if you don't 'get' something – rap, ballet, *Friends*,
TikTok – you still do your best to join in.

... You insist on the silly family traditions that
everyone loves and passes on.

... You let your kids make mistakes because you know they'll
learn from them. From scraping knees to denting cars...

... You kept the refrigerator shut, guarded the thermostat
and recommended putting on an extra jumper before
anyone had even heard of Greta Thunberg.

... You're honest, especially when you don't like what
someone (your daughter in particular...) is wearing.

... You don't mind forgoing a beer to pick your kids up
from a party – and know to wait out of sight.

... You never stop believing in your children,
especially when they don't believe in themselves.

Dad Dancing
IN 10 AWKWARD STEPS

Dads who stay off the dance floor to spare their family embarrassment really are killjoys. They need to get up on their feet, enjoy themselves and provide the entertainment! Here are 10 great tips for dancing like only a dad can. Some say it's natural, some say it's learned...

1. It doesn't matter what the song/genre/rhythm is, you must do the same dance regardless.

2. Choose your weapon early on. You have two choices: (1) the dad shuffle or (2) the all-out-knock-everyone-else-out-of-the-room. Either way, keep it simple.

3. Jackets should remain on when you move onto the dance floor. They are a vital prop for when the DJ spins Tom Jones' 'You Can Leave Your Hat On'.

4. If you've chosen the dad shuffle, your feet shouldn't move forwards or backwards, only side to side. To reduce friction and ensure a smooth shuffle, it is recommended that trainers are avoided.

5. Make eye contact with your significant other (if they've not left you to your own devices yet). You've got this! Think David Attenborough and the courtship dance of a blue-footed booby.

6. Don't try too hard and don't attempt the latest dance moves (especially when 'latest' means 20 years ago). Listen to the music and do whatever feels natural...

7. Beware of relying on beer to lose your inhibitions. It may lubricate the joints, but if you want to look like a pro on any videos that get posted on social media, go steady on the sauce. (And don't dance with a drink in your hand. Two words: spills and slips.)

8. Spatial awareness is everything if you want to remain on good terms with your fellow dancers.

9. Take these suggestions lightly – basically, dad dancing is impossible to get wrong. In fact, the more wrong your dancing, the better you're doing.

10. Make sure that your flies are done up before engaging in any of the above.

When Mum says 'No'
DAD SAYS...

... a great, big, fat YES! One of the best things about dads is that they agree to things that mums don't hesitate to put the kibosh on.

....

Money... Mum thinks you're going to spend it unwisely. Dad knows that frivolous spending is one of life's essentials. After all, he's taught you everything you know.

11

Car... Mum assumes the worst – that you'll be irresponsible and will be calling at 4am when you've run out of petrol or have a flat tyre. Dad knows how important owning your own car is and what a difference it makes to your life... your love life, mainly.

New trainers... Mum says you should make do with the Dunlop Green Flash trainers you've had since school. Dad knows that he's gone way beyond fancy trainers being able to make him cool, so is more than happy to live vicariously through you.

Mobile phone upgrade... Mum wonders why you can't just manage with the landline and by talking to your friends at school. Dad knows that if you don't have the latest phone you may as well say goodbye to that lucrative YouTube career that's going to pay for his retirement.

No vegetables... Mum only has your best interests at heart and wants to make sure you're filled with green goodness. Dad has been eating Mum's soggy veg for 20 years and has never been brave enough to resist. He salutes you.

Staying out past midnight... Mum will be twitching the curtains and won't get any sleep until you're safely home. Dad remembers that the fun doesn't really start until the witching hour – that's how he met your mother.

Top Ten DAD SUPERPOWERS

Even the most unassuming dads have superpowers. No invisibility cloaks, webs shooting from their fingers and definitely no lycra (thank goodness), but dads have the knack of using their awesome skills at exactly the right moment.

1. They always know the right thing to say. Even when you call at midnight in a state about something happening at work the next day, dads find the calming words to set you back on the right track.

2. They know that nothing is too big or too small for them to drop everything for you. No "Give me five minutes" or "Just let me do this" – dads don't need to get changed in a telephone box, they're ready for anything.

3. Whilst dads might be useless at reading the minds of their partners, they're brilliant at knowing exactly what you're thinking. Not always a good thing, but when there's something you ought to be telling them and aren't (for example, that you drove the car into the garage door), they'll wheedle it out of you in a flash.

4. Dads can tell a joke that's so very, very bad that even the Grand Canyon would crumble under the sheer awfulness of it.

5. The ability to memorize every piece of scrap, junk, bit and bob that they've ever collected because they might need it one day. Of course, they will need it and for five minutes everyone stops laughing at the state of dad's garage.

6. They have an incredible talent for falling asleep instantly, regardless of where they are and the noise levels – a superpower shared only with cats and dogs. Possibly a defence mechanism and often deployed at family gatherings.

7. If dads say "no" (and think they mean it), they have an amazing ability to completely give in without letting you feel like you've won.

8. They can push you out of your comfort zone without you even realizing it. Remember when your dad took the training wheels off your bike and you thought he was still holding you up? (He wasn't.) And when you were learning to swim and you could never quite reach your dad's outstretched arms? (He was moving backwards.)

9. Dads can tolerate anything disgusting that you produce. From your nappies in the early days through to the morning after the night before when you went to your first house party, there's very little you can do that will turn your father's stomach.

10. Dads know that they don't actually need superpowers to be a super dad but are very happy for you to believe it (that will be their power of mind control at work).

Things to do on
THE TOILET

... other than the obvious. Tired of being moaned at for spending too long in the smallest room in the house? Time to start using your time on the toilet productively. No one can argue with that!

....

Start a podcast or a blog. If you've got something interesting to say/write, let the world know. (A blog might be better than recording a podcast in the toilet – funny acoustics.)

Take an online course. What have you always wanted to learn? Choose something from one of the many free courses available online – who knows where it will take you?

Edit the photo book you've never got round to. Remember that family holiday of a lifetime three years ago? The one you promised you'd immortalize in a photo book to treasure forever?

Write your bucket list. If there's something you've always wanted to do but haven't got round to doing it, stop pondering and start planning. Nothing gets things done like a to-do list.

Chair yoga. It's a thing. Google it. Go to the toilet and get fit!

Write a letter. With paper (ideally not toilet paper) and a pen. When did you last take the time to write a proper letter?

Clean up your inbox. Newsletters you've subscribed to on the promise of winning beer and 30-day plank challenges never started. Time to hit the little dustbin button.

Meditate. Just 10 minutes of meditation a day can bring positive benefits. Reduce stress and anxiety – and all before a ring forms on your bottom.

SOCCER

Most people know a little bit about 'the beautiful game', whether they like it or not. But if you've only absorbed a few useless facts by osmosis, you're going to be in a pickle if you're called up for the Dad's XI. Luckily, like a player rolling around on the floor claiming a foul, you can fake it...

1. The offside rule is one of the most difficult rules to understand. The good news is that no one really gets it! So, in one sentence: Being offside occurs when a player goes behind the line of opposing defenders before the ball has been kicked to them. Clear?

2. You cannot pick up the ball. You cannot pick it up and run with it. You certainly cannot (legally) bundle other players to the floor. This is not rugby.

3. A penalty kick occurs when a player gets wrongly knocked over near their goal. Don't volunteer to take a penalty kick – it is VERY important and should only be taken by someone who's confident about kicking a ball in the right direction.

4. 4-4-2 is a basic soccer formation. You'll notice it adds up to 10 rather than 11. That's because there are 10 players plus the goalkeeper. The first '4' in the 4-4-2 means four defenders, the players in front of the goalkeeper. Then there are four midfielders – they attack and defend, and link the defenders with the two forwards, the players most expected to score goals.

5. The goalkeeper always wears a different colour shirt so that the referee can spot them easily. This will also help you spot who not to kick the ball at if you're trying to score a goal.

6. Soccer players are famous for over-exaggerating injuries, also known as 'diving'. It's best avoided unless you've turned in a previous Oscar-winning performance. If you haven't, you'll just look pathetic.

7. Know your soccer heroes. David Beckham, underwear model, husband to pop star-turned-fashion-designer and dad to Instagram-friendly kids, was once a famous English midfielder. Yes, really.

8. A match lasts 90 minutes. Do conserve some energy – the referee can add extra time if there have been injuries. In some cup games, another 30 minutes can be added if no one has scored the most goals after the original 90 minutes. Sometimes, a match can end with a penalty shootout. If this happens, the previous 120 minutes are irrelevant.

9. In the unlikely event you score a goal, you MUST have a victory dance choreographed in advance.

10. Choose a favourite team to support and stick to it. There are some key facts you must know in case anyone starts a conversation with you about your team: Who is their manager? Which league are they in? How is their season going? After that, change the subject.

Dad JOKES

What did the daddy buffalo say to his son
as he was leaving the house?

Bison!

Son: Dad, what's it like to have the best son
in the whole world?

Dad: I don't know, you'll have to ask Grandma!

There was a dad who tried to keep his partner happy through
labour by telling jokes, but she didn't laugh once...

It was the delivery.

It's a
FACT!

Male rheas are the super dads of the bird world. The only male in a group of up to 12 females, the father rhea incubates up to 50 eggs for 40 days. He then raises the chicks completely on his own and will chase anything, including females, away from his chicks.

Ramajit Raghav from India is believed to be the oldest dad in the world. He was 96 years old when his 52-year-old wife gave birth to a boy in 2010. Raghav took his time – he was single until he was in his eighties!

Male seahorses are the only male animals that can become pregnant. They are presented with around 50–1,500 eggs by the female for fertilizing. They then carry the eggs for several weeks until they're ready to hatch.

The tradition of a father 'giving away' the bride comes from the historical belief that a daughter was the property of her father. By giving his daughter away, it signified that he would no longer have control over her, her well-being or her possessions, and that her husband would take on the responsibilities of the father.

Patri is Latin for 'father'. You'll find it used as the root of many related words, for example: patriarch, patrician, patriot, patron, patronize and paternity.

Expectant dads can experience something called a 'sympathy pregnancy'. The symptoms are similar to that of the pregnant mother and include weight gain, nausea and changing hormone levels.

Dos and don'ts of
DAD FASHION

Dad fashion can be a minefield.
Do you want to look cool, preppy, clever
or to just not stick out like a sore thumb?
You just need some basic tips...

Do

Wear jeans that fit you well. While 'mum jeans' are fashionable, 'dad jeans' aren't (unless you're not a dad and are wearing them ironically). Step away from baggy legs and loose waistbands – straight-legged and high-waisted jeans give plenty of movement AND signal you're on-trend.

Check out brands before you buy. Brands that look cool to you in the shop might be the laughing stock of your children (who will always be trendier than you).

Iron your clothes. Creased doesn't say cool and effortless; it says scruffy and lazy.

Keep your wardrobe manageable. Have key pieces that mix and match with each other. If you can get dressed in the dark and still look great, you've cracked it.

Wear colours that you like. If you like black and navy, buy black and navy. It's about wearing what you're comfortable in. Life's too short to be hiding behind your family, awkwardly sporting a Hawaiian shirt they chose for you.

Don't

Wear big logos. Keep your logos discreet and classy.

Be the talk of the school run by pushing the boundaries of the acceptable. Once talked about by the mum cliques, it will take years to live down.

Unbutton your shirt too far down. Even if it's an excruciatingly hot day.

Tuck in sweatshirts, jumpers or T-shirts. No, no, no. The only thing it's okay to tuck in is shirts!

Wear your phone on a holster on your belt. There will never be an occasion when you need to access your phone so rapidly that it warrants this fashion faux pas.

Wear white socks with dark shoes and dark trousers. When in doubt, match your sock colour to your trouser colour. (AND DO WEAR SOCKS WITH SHOES! You're not in *Miami Vice*.)

Be tempted to wear novelty ties and waistcoats. They don't make you look fun and crazy. It's the quickest way to ruin a good suit (and to not be invited back for a second interview).

Dads on the BIG SCREEN

A list of great films about dads needs a book all of its own. Dads are so brilliant, we just can't stop making movies about them. But beware, not all of them challenge the stereotype that dads are terrible at looking after children when left to their own devices!

Dad (1989) – Three generations – grandfather, father and son – come together to live under the same roof and finally establish a true connection. Prepare for some tears.

Father of the Bride (1991) – A comedy about a father (Steve Martin) who has a hard time letting go of his daughter before her wedding.

Three Men and a Baby (1987) – What happens when three bachelors find a baby on their doorstep?

Field of Dreams (1989) – Ray begins a quest to turn his ordinary cornfield into a place where dreams can come true.

Daddy Day Care (2003) – Two men get laid off from their jobs and become stay-at-home fathers. They become inspired to set up a new day-care centre.

On Golden Pond (1981) – An estranged daughter goes to stay with her family to mend her relationship with her cantankerous father before it's too late.

We Bought a Zoo (2011) – A young widower and journalist takes on a new adventure when he purchases a run-down wildlife reserve and moves there with his two children.

Mr Mom (1983) – A dad takes over the job of caring for his three kids. (Yes, again.)

Mrs Doubtfire (1993) – A hilarious but heartfelt story of how far a father will go to care for his children.

Star Wars: The Empire Strikes Back (1980) – "Luke, I am your father." (Need we say more?)

The Pursuit of Happyness (2006) – The true story of a struggling single dad who dreams of a better life for his son.

Indiana Jones and the Last Crusade (1989) – Indiana Jones tries to rescue his missing father, who was kidnapped by Nazis while searching for the Holy Grail.

All about YOU

"You can tell what was the best year of your father's life,
because they seem to freeze that clothing style and ride it out."

JERRY SEINFELD

"The older I get, the smarter my father seems to get."

TIM RUSSERT

"Life doesn't come with an instruction book
– that's why we have fathers."

H. JACKSON BROWN JR

Bluff it: DIY

Thanks to stereotypes that just won't go away, there's a lot of pressure on dads to be good at certain things. One of these is DIY. Under the banner of DIY comes flat-pack furniture building, fixing things (plumbing, electrical and other things that could kill the unqualified) and using the internet to bypass a proper builder and build your own extension.

1. Want to look the part, even if you've never drilled a hole in your life? Buy a tool belt. Whether you need a screwdriver or a hammer, you'll be faster to the draw than John Wayne.

2. YouTube is your friend. Whatever your DIY task in hand, it's guaranteed that Colin of Calgary or Randy of Rhode Island will have posted a video about it. These how-to videos run through jobs step by step, whether you simply want to rewire a plug or recreate Brooklyn Bridge in your backyard.

3. If you're redecorating over a dark colour, always paint the walls with a lighter primer/undercoat first. Not only will this reduce the number of coats you'll need to hide the old colour but, if you're lucky, you may even find your partner prefers minimalist white to 'Elephant Buttock Grey'.

4. A simple spirit level can make any job look good. Nothing says 'bodged' more than a shelf at a jaunty angle or walking uphill on a new floor.

5. Flat-pack furniture. Don't rush, play it cool – preparation is everything. Make some space, take all the components out of the box and lay them out neatly. Check all the pieces are there (this will save on frustration later in the process). Don't be tempted to have a beer or a glass of wine before you start.

6. Second only to a tool belt is a workbench. It is well worth investing in one, if only to make it look like you know what you're doing. It's great for clamping wood to when you're cutting, and it will prevent any more incidents of sawing through the kitchen table.

7. While DIY electrics is not recommended, DIY plumbing poses less of a risk to your safety. Remember, though, it does have the potential to cause damage to your home and your heating system. Most important of all is to familiarize yourself with the location of your stopcock (it stops the water pouring out).

8. MDF (medium-density fibreboard) is no longer considered the material of TV home-makeover show bodge jobs. It's an inexpensive option for carpentry projects and works well for shelving and storage. Don't be tempted to start your DIY journey using expensive wood when MDF will do.

9. Always visit DIY and hardware stores alone. It's the perfect opportunity to chat to an expert – and no one will know when you pass their expertise off as your own.

10. Remember, if you think a job is too much for you, it undoubtedly is. Calling in a professional can save your sanity, your limbs and your marriage.

10 reasons kids are INCREDIBLE!

In a book all about dads, let's not forget who made them who they are – their children! Some would even say they're the power behind the throne. Here's a reminder why ankle-biters are absolutely kidtastic...

1. They keep you young. Not only do you get a chance to build Lego again, but studies have shown that people with children have lower blood pressure than those without – although it might not feel like it when you're trying to get them all into the car.

2. They put the brakes on your overspend. There's nothing like a bill for three pairs of new school shoes to make you think twice about upgrading your own wardrobe.

3. They ensure you understand what's in fashion. They'll educate you just enough so that you aren't an embarrassment to them in public.

4. Their taste in music confirms that your own music collection is a fine example of when people used to listen to proper music with real instruments.

5. They teach you things you didn't know and would be scared to Google. ("Is that even a thing?" "There was no such thing in my day." "Do people really do *that*?")

6. They're your passport to visit all the places you've missed since you were a kid but are too embarrassed to visit as an adult on your own.

7. They remind you what unconditional love is – how to accept it and how to give it.

8. They make you laugh – often at them, but mostly at yourself. Life's too short to take yourself too seriously.

9. They're a great alibi. Don't want to accept an invitation to a colleague's leaving party? Just say you need to pick the kids up from somewhere/someone/something.

10. They're going to look after you when you're old and decrepit. As you pop your teeth in a glass, you'll realize all the time and money you spent on them was worth it!

Dadisms

Dads always have a little nugget of brilliance for every occasion. Only the best kind of wisdom has the power to stop wayward offspring in their tracks!

....

"I'm not sleeping, I'm just resting my eyes."

"If they told you to jump off a cliff, would you?"

"Don't tell your mother."

"Don't make me stop the car!"

"Pull my finger..."

"If it's not where you think it is, it's where you think it isn't."

"Shut the door – we're not heating the street!"

"What did your mother say?"

"A little dirt never hurt anyone."

"Am I talking to a brick wall?"

"You're not leaving this house dressed like that!"

"When you have children of your own, you'll understand."

"It's just what I've always wanted!"

"Don't throw that out! We can use that."

"Were you raised in a barn?"

"Do you think I'm made of money?"

"'Hey' is for horses."

"Because I said so, that's why."

"I don't need to read the instructions."

What kids
THINK...

Ever wondered what kids are thinking but might never tell their dad? Rest assured, it's so lovely that it could bring a tear to your eye.

....

Dad, I really appreciate all your advice – it makes absolute sense.

I'm not angry at you, I'm just finding things tough at the moment.

I may not have listened to you at the time, but I want you to know that it turned out just like you said.

DADTASTIC – WHY YOU'RE SO AWESOME

I'm grateful for all the sacrifices – large and small
– you've made for me.

If I'm worried about something, I think "What would Dad do?"

You're not embarrassing; in fact, I'm incredibly proud of you.

Without you, Dad, I'd have found it so much harder
to be the person I am today.

I couldn't have asked for a better role model.

For every time you picked me up in the car and I
didn't have to get the bus – thank you.

I wish I'd listened when you said my boyfriend/girlfriend
wasn't good enough for me – you were right, as always.

If you weren't so brilliant at calming Mum down, I'd have
been in a whole lot of trouble – more than once!

I'm glad you made me say my 'pleases and thank yous', even
though it drove me mad and embarrassed me in public.

Thank you for letting me make my own mistakes at times.
I know it was hard for you.

I hope that my children will love me as much as I love you.

The relationship COACH

Sex, love and relationships can be difficult for any parent to talk about. Whether it's introducing the birds and the bees or dealing out some hard facts about heartbreak, dads have a certain way with words.

"Dad, where do babies come from?"

DAD SAYS:

"I've told you about the stork. Now go and ask
your mum if you want more detail."

"You're covering this at school next term. Best wait until then."

"That's a great question. Tell me – what do you think?"

"Hold on a minute, why do you need to know that?!??!"

"Dad, I think they're Mr/Miss Right..."

DAD SAYS:

"Do they look after you and make you feel safe?"

"If you can break wind in front of each other, it must be love."

"Live with them and then you'll know for sure."

"I can see how happy you are and that makes me happy.
But if they make you sad..."

"But you've only been dating for five years!"

"Dad, they've dumped me!"

DAD SAYS:

"I never liked them anyway. They weren't good enough for you."

"They're an idiot. You'll always be amazing to me."

"If they try to contact you, tell them your dad
has a shovel and an alibi."

"Thank goodness. I never trust anyone who wears shoes like that."

"Do I need to tell the new lodger that they
can't have your room after all?"

All about YOU

"A father carries pictures where his money used to be."
STEVE MARTIN

"Fatherhood is the greatest thing that could ever happen.
You can't explain it until it happens – it's like telling someone
what water feels like before they've ever swam in it."
MICHAEL BUBLÉ

"When my father didn't have my hand, he had my back."
LINDA POINDEXTER

Bluff it:
GOLF

If you believe gift catalogues, EVERY dad plays golf. Why else would it be possible to buy them golf tees to suit any occasion, whether it be Christmas, a birthday or Father's Day? But if you're not a golfer, how the devil can you fake it when you get that invitation you just can't say "no" to?

1. A 'bogey' is a score of one over par of the hole. (The 'par' is the average number of times you'd expect to have to hit the little white ball before it goes in the hole.) All you really need to know is that it's different to the bogey you remove from a child's nose.

2. V-neck jumpers and nylon pleated trousers are de rigeur for all serious golfers. The more checks or plaid you can introduce into your trouser material, the more seriously you'll be taken. Failure to adhere to etiquette – for example, the scandalous wearing of jeans – will result in an expensive trip to the golf shop to buy trousers you'll never wear again.

3. If someone calls you a 'duffer', it is not a term of endearment. The other person is referring to your mediocre or poor golfing abilities.

4. FACT: you will hit a lot of balls into the bushes. To avoid wasting other players' time and becoming the most irritating person they've ever played a round with, make sure you have lots of spare balls so you can call off the search party early.

5. Do not talk whilst someone else is swinging. Golfers take their hobby – sorry, *sport* – incredibly seriously and must focus as if what they're doing matters more than, say, climate change.

6. Never ever ask where the hole with the windmill is. Or the one where the ball goes in the crocodile's mouth and re-emerges from its butt. That would just be crazy (golf).

7. To hit the ball a long way, you need to use the stick (club) called the 'driver'. Then there are different 'irons', depending on how far you want to hit the ball. You'll use the 'wedge' a lot – it's the one that gets your ball out of a bunker. If you ever get close enough to the green – where you'll find the hole – you will need the 'putter'.

8. In the US, 5% of all lightning deaths and injuries happen on golf courses. Check the weather before you play. Just sayin'.

9. Yell 'FORE' if your ball is anywhere close to heading towards another group. Nearly getting hit will make golfers extremely angry. And you don't want to see them when they're angry...

10. Remember, if you're terrified and are playing terribly, you can still have fun! Laugh off that shot where you fell flat on your back. Even the best golfers have bad days. Look at Tiger Woods: he's had A LOT of bad days, both on and off the course.

Dad
JOKES

My dad told a chemistry joke but he got no reaction.

Yesterday, I was washing the car with my son.
He said, "Dad, can't you just use a sponge?"

My daughter just shrieked at me, "Dad! You haven't listened to a word I've said, have you?" What an odd way to begin a conversation.

If you've never left a store carrying your screaming child like a surfboard, you've never been a dad.

Things dads would
NEVER SAY

Dads say it like it is, but sometimes it's not what their kids want to hear. If a dad were to say any of the following, everyone in earshot would have to pick their jaws up off the ground.

....

"Please can you turn your music up?"

"Why don't you take my car? And here's my credit card too."

"No, no, you take the remote. It's all yours."

"I think we're lost. Let's stop and ask for directions."

"Your bad attitude is brilliant. I love it."

"I'm going to be away for the whole weekend.
Why don't you throw a party?"

"Isn't your skirt a bit too long?"

"Why did you get a weekend job? I've got plenty
of money that I'm happy for you to spend."

"Father's Day? Oh, it's no big deal."

"I know exactly what to buy your mother for our anniversary."

"Great idea not to wear a coat tonight. It's freezing outside but,
wow, coats are so bulky on a night out."

"There's no way I can fix that. We'll have to buy a brand new one."

"You're growing up much too slowly."

"Eleven o'clock seems a bit early to leave a party.
How about I pick you up at 3am?"

"Of course it's okay for you to borrow my favourite sweater
and leave it in the park."

Dad, please
DON'T EVER...

... stop dancing at family parties (but please do see page 8).

... grow a moustache that needs to be curled and waxed.

... forget that you promised you'd teach me how to drive.

... stop trying to embarrass me – secretly, I find it funny.

... throw out your old clothes. They'll come back
in fashion and I've got my eye on them.

... forget that I'm your favourite child. Just remember
who it was that bought you this book.

... doubt that you're the most amazing, fantastic
and brilliant dad ever.

Dads on THE PAGE

Whether it's a hefty novel or a light-hearted look at the perils of being a new dad, there is a book for every dad need. So, it's time for dads to put their feet up, pull on their favourite loungewear and slippers, and settle down with a cracking read...

To Kill a Mockingbird by Harper Lee – Atticus Finch, a local lawyer, is a single father who not only tackles household challenges but also defends a wrongly accused black man in a racist US town. Finch is one of the strongest father figures in modern literature.

Horton the Elephant by Dr Seuss — An elephant teaches dads everywhere to mean what they say and say what they mean.

The Twelve Lives of Samuel Hawley by Hannah Tinti – A novel about the lengths we go to in order to protect our family.

The Road by Cormac McCarthy – The story of one man fighting for his survival and the survival of his child.

Man and Boy by Tony Parsons – A man comes to terms with his life bringing up his son alone, and learns what words like 'love' and 'family' really mean.

The Godfather by Mario Puzo – THE classic story of blackmail, murder and family. As Vito Corleone nears the end of a long life of crime, his sons step up to manage the family business.

This is Ridiculous This is Amazing by Jason Good – A funny collection of lists to help new dads through every parenting situation, including 'Games You Can Play While Lying Down'.

Dreams from My Father: A Story of Race and Inheritance by Barack Obama – A portrait of a young man asking big questions about identity and belonging.

To Me, He Was Just Dad: Stories of Growing Up with Famous Fathers by Joshua David Stein – Children of famous dads share a private perspective of a public figure and explore the idea of what it means to be a father.

Esther the Wonder Pig by Steve Jenkins and Derek Walter – A true story of how Steve and Derek got more than they bargained for when the mini-piglet they adopted grew into a full-sized 600-pound sow.

Pops: Fatherhood in Pieces by Michael Chabon – A collection of humorous and heartfelt essays on the meaning of fatherhood.

Sh*t My Dad Says by Justin Halpern – Quotes by Halpern's father on various subjects, originally posted by the author on Twitter.

Home Game: An Accidental Guide to Fatherhood by Michael Lewis – How different is the idea of fatherhood from what it's actually like? The author talks about what he thought he was supposed to be feeling and doing as a father – and what was really going on in his day-to-day life.

It's a
FACT!

The first ever Father's Day was celebrated on 19 June 1910 in the United States. It was originally invented by a daughter who wanted to celebrate her father, who was a widowed Civil War veteran with six children and a farm. In 1972, President Nixon signed the holiday into law.

The word 'dad' dates back to the 1500s, possibly even earlier. We're not completely sure where and how the word originated, but it's believed it comes from baby talk.

In the 18th century, Russian man Feodor Vassilyev set a record for the most children fathered to one woman. The couple are reported to have had 69 children, including four sets of quadruplets, seven sets of triplets, and 16 pairs of twins.

A 2014 study published in *Psychological Science* found that fathers who helped with household chores had daughters who aspired to less traditionally female-dominated jobs and higher-paying careers.

In 1912, American Halsey Taylor invented the drinking water fountain. It was a tribute to his father, who died from typhoid fever after drinking from a contaminated public water supply in 1896.

The male Darwin frog hatches his eggs in a pouch in his mouth. He can continue to eat at the same time. When his tadpoles lose their tails and become tiny frogs, they jump out of his mouth.

Songs
ABOUT DAD

It's not surprising that the special relationship between dads and their kids has inspired multiple songs – some sad, some happy, but always heartfelt. Our top 10 (in no particular order) will have every dad up and shuffling...

'Unforgettable' – Nat King Cole and Natalie Cole

'Song for Dad' – Keith Urban

'Beautiful Boy (Darling Boy)' – John Lennon

'They Don't Make 'Em Like My Daddy Anymore' – Loretta Lynn

'My Father's Eyes' – Eric Clapton

'Dance with my Father' – Luther Vandross

'Lullaby (Goodnight My Angel)' – Billy Joel

'Papa's Got a Brand New Bag' – James Brown

'Cat's in the Cradle' – Harry Chapin

'The Best Day' – George Strait

And two bonus tracks:

'Father and Daughter' – Paul Simon

'Father and Son' – Cat Stevens

Sweet little
WHITE LIES

Not all lies are bad. Some are to protect
us or to stop us doing something stupid.
Some are for self-preservation – and these
are the lies dads like best of all. If dad
says it's true, then it must be. By the time
we reach the age to realize it isn't, we can
understand exactly why they said it.

Lie #1: If you sit too close to the television it will ruin your eyes.

Truth: You're totally blocking my view and it's impossible to follow what's going on. Move!

Lie #2: Where did you come from? Well, the stork brought you.

Truth: It's much easier to tell you this and it will postpone some really tricky questions until you're 18, at least.

Lie #3: It's not unfair. Your sister isn't staying up later than you – she'll be going to bed straight after you do.

Truth: Your sister is 21! I don't even know where she is, let alone what time she's going to bed.

Lie #4: No, you can't play games on my tablet – I left it at Grandma's house.

Truth: My tablet only has 3% battery left and as soon as you're out of the room, I'm watching another episode of *Squid Game.*

Lie #5: If the wind changes when you're pulling that face, your face will stay like that forever.

Truth: Your grandad told me that when I was five and I didn't leave the house when it was windy until I was 10. Other people need to experience this terror too.

Lie #6: *Fifty Shades of Grey* is an incredibly dull documentary about someone deciding what colour to paint their house.

Truth: I can't believe your mother left that DVD out!

Lie #7: The lady who owns the internet switches it off at 6pm every day.

Truth: I've finally figured out how to set restrictions on the wi-fi but I'd rather put scorpions in my bed than tell you that.

Lie #8: If you pick your nose and eat it, you'll get a huge bogey ball in your tummy and need to go to hospital.

Truth: Why do I tell you this lie when I know full well that if you don't eat them, you'll just stick them on the furniture.

Lie #9: If you pick a dandelion, you'll wet the bed.

Truth: I don't want you to touch something that has probably been peed on by a dog. You're going to want to hold my hand and I don't have any wipes with me.

Lie #10: You'll understand when you're older.

Truth: No, you won't. I still haven't figured it out and I'm 48! I'm just saying it so you stop asking and I can avoid discussing it any further.

Our hero:
DAD VERSUS BEAST

Dad versus Wolf

In 2019, a Canadian dad saved his family from a wolf that tore into their tent whilst they were camping in Banff National Park. Putting himself between his family and the wolf, the dad tried to pin the wolf down, but it started to drag him away. Luckily, another hero dad arrived on the scene and kicked the wolf, startling it enough that it let go. Dads are heroes AND guardian angels!

Dad versus Bear

In a US national park, a dad awoke to hear his teenage son screaming. The shocked dad saw his son's head in a bear's jaws and the bear dragging him across the ground. Desperate to save his son, the man jumped onto the bear's back, hit it in the face and then threw rocks at it until it let go. The dad and his son had to hike several miles to reach help. Thankfully, the son made a full recovery.

Dad versus Snake

A dad in Australia saved his four-year-old son from the jaws of a 15-foot-long python. The huge snake attacked the boy in the garden of the family's home during a party. Finding the snake biting his son and trying to drag him into the bushes, the brave dad hit the snake on the head, briefly stunning it. Unbelievably, the snake attacked the boy again, so the dad grabbed its mouth and pulled its jaws apart until it let go. Finally, he grabbed the snake's tail and his son was able to make his escape.

All about
YOU

"A child enters your home and for the next twenty years makes so much noise you can hardly stand it. The child departs, leaving the house so silent you think you are going mad."

JOHN ANDREWS HOLMES

"I have a stepson, five biological children, grandchildren, and a couple of great-grandchildren. And the treasure of all this: I still get a little jump every time I hear 'Dad'."

LARRY KING

"Dads are most ordinary men turned by love into heroes, adventurers, story-tellers, and singers of songs."

PAM BROWN

Bluff it: FISHING

Just like playing golf, men are born with a natural ability to fish, right? They know how to cast a line before they learn to crawl. Truth is, not as many dads are avid anglers as the greetings card companies like to think. Here's a dad's guide to faking it...

65

1. Should a fellow fisherman refer to their (or your) 'tackle', do not be alarmed or embarrassed. 'Tackle' is the collective word for equipment used by anglers and includes your rods, reels, bait, nets, etc., etc.

2. Always looks behind you and to the side before casting your line (the bit when you wave your rod in the air to get the line and hook into the water). If you don't, you risk catching another angler's hat, a small child or, worse still, an overhead power line.

3. Fishing can be as challenging or as relaxing an activity as you choose to make it. Fishing tends to be a whole-day experience (at least), so choose a level you can sustain.

4. If you get a bite, play it cool. Overexcitement will simply give away that you're an imposter. Whooping will scare away all the other fish in the vicinity and invite the unbridled anger of all those fishing around you.

5. Remember to wet your hand before you handle a fish – it will help protect their scales and the mucus that covers them. It also makes them more hilariously slippery and provides the fish with the opportunity to make a fool of you.

6. What's the rudest thing you can do on the river? Just try starting fishing downstream from another angler. It's like

jumping a bus queue but a thousand times worse. If you survive, don't expect them to offer you any friendly advice.

7. All anglers have a lucky hat. If you wear a thermal bobble hat on your first fishing outing and land 20 fish, you'll find yourself having to wear that hat forever, whether its winter or a heatwave.

8. If your fishing companions appear to be consuming too much beer, virtuously point out the health benefits of fishing. Being outdoors increases your vitamin D (which helps regulate the amount of calcium and phosphate in your body, keeping your bones and teeth healthy) and boosts your immune system. However, it doesn't cancel out too much alcohol.

9. Fishermen (especially those fishing at sea) are superstitious people. They believe that you shouldn't talk whilst fishing because the fish can hear you and you won't catch anything. So, here's a tip: when asked a tricky fishing question you have no clue about, just raise your finger to your lips and say "Shhhhh…"

10. You've spent the whole of your life telling yourself that 'size isn't everything'. Remember, when you're fishing, size is absolutely EVERYTHING. Be prepared for lots of men comparing the size of their catch.

Top 10
DAD BEAUTY PRODUCTS

Are you a dad struggling to find space in the bathroom cabinet for all the soaps-on-ropes and unwanted gift sets you receive at Christmas? It's time to bin them all and start afresh. To save you staring at an empty space wondering whether toothpaste doubles up as deodorant, here's a handy list of what to restock with.

1. **Shaving gel.** Things have moved on since the days of shaving foam, when your morning routine made you look like you'd been ambushed by a clown with a custard pie. Choose a shaving gel that contains moisturizers (look for the word 'soothing') and you'll save vital minutes by not needing to moisturize separately!

2. **Invigorating shower wash.** Anything that invigorates, revitalizes or energizes first thing in the morning must be a good thing – especially when tequila isn't an option.

3. **Tweezers.** For everything that sprouts out of your face and back. Especially for dads who find the thought of waxing horrific.

4. **Nasal hair trimmer.** See item 3 above. The classic dad gadget that's perfect for those who are scared of tweezers, let alone waxing.

5. **Muscle gel.** Not to help grow muscles, simply to soothe them. Particularly restorative after a hard day's golfing, fishing, playing soccer or doing DIY – or all those manly activities the patriarchy expects men to be doing.

6. **Anti-fatigue eye serum.** Probably the most expensive piece of kit. Vital whilst your children are aged 0–18 and you don't want to be mistaken for their great-grandfather.

7. **Old-fashioned shaving kit.** Such a kit generally includes a razor, shaving cream (in an unfathomable solid block), stand (that keeps falling over), shaving brush (for dusting dandruff off shoulders) and a shaving bowl (for storing bits and bobs in). That's right – it's useless for shaving but you should still have one.

8. **Beard moisturizer.** Does your beard look like it's home to mice and bears? Could you use it to get last night's burnt bolognese off the bottom of the pan? Then you need to smooth and tame it! Keep up with the hipsters and groom your beard harder than you'd groom a show dog. Beard moisturizer will make your beard so ruly and soft, you won't be able to stop stroking it.

9. **Deodorant.** Sounds obvious, but often overlooked! If you have just one thing in your (under)armoury, it's deodorant. Just remember that the ones promising 48-hour protection don't really last longer than the others, so reapply liberally during the day.

10. **Aftershave.** Every dad's opportunity to leave their mark in a room long after they've exited. Just make sure it's a good impression you leave behind, so avoid applying too much or the smell will be overpowering. Don't make people swoon for all the wrong reasons.

Tricky question
CHEAT SHEET

Dads are heroes but they don't know EVERYTHING. However, we like to believe they do, so here's a helping hand for dads faced with tough questions about the universe, life and everything else (well, some of it).

Q: What is the universe made of?

A: 5% of the universe is made up of atoms. The remaining 95% is comprised of two shadowy entities – dark matter and dark energy.

Q: Why do we dream?

A: I don't know. Scientists still don't know! We do know that dreams could play a role in memory, learning and emotions.

Q: Can you dig a hole to the other side of the world?

A: No, it's pretty much an engineering impossibility. Even if it were possible, you'd have to pass through temperatures that are hotter than the surface of the sun.

Q: Why don't all fish die when lightning hits the sea?

A: Seawater conducts electricity and spreads it out in all directions. Fish would probably only experience a small current passing through them and therefore wouldn't die.

Q: How much does the sky weigh?

A: It weighs roughly the same as 570,000,000,000,000 adult Indian elephants.

Q: Why is water wet?

A: When you have water on you, it evaporates into the air. Evaporation produces cooling. The feeling of wetness is actually coldness.

Q: How do clouds float when they're full of water?

A: The water and ice particles in clouds are too tiny to be affected by gravity. As a result, clouds appear to float in the air.

Q: What is infinity?

A: Infinity is something that has no end. Imagine travelling on and on, trying hard to get there, but never actually getting there.

Q: Why is blood red?

A: Blood is red because it's made up of cells that are red. It looks red because of how the chemical reaction between the iron in our blood and the oxygen reflects light.

Q: How does the internet work?

A: The internet is a basic computer network that moves information from one place to another. There are millions of servers on the internet that store information. Routers connect all the different systems together.

Q: Why is the sky blue?

A: As sunlight travels towards us, it hits gas and dust particles in the air and light is scattered in all directions. The colour blue in sunlight gets scattered more than other colours so we see mostly blue in the sky.

Q: Which came first, the chicken or the egg?

A: Hmmm. At some point when there were no chickens, two birds that were almost-but-not-quite chickens mated and laid an egg that hatched into the first chicken. So, the egg came first. BUT you could also argue that the first 'real' chicken had to be alive to lay what could be called a 'chicken's egg'. In this case, the chicken came first!

Don't ask YOUR KIDS

We've covered the questions kids ask to make their dads' heads explode, but what about the other way round? What questions should you never ask your little darlings at any age? These are the questions dads shouldn't just tiptoe around but should swerve around at high speed if they want to retain their dadtastic crown. Sometimes, you just don't want to know the answer.

"How are you going to pay for that?"

"Who do you love more? Me or your phone?"

"Why are you single?"

"How many boyfriends/girlfriends/partners have you had?"

"I don't embarrass you, do I?"

"What did you do last night?"

"Did you wash your hands before eating that?"

"Can I tell you what I think?"

"What kind of dad am I?"

"What's the most dangerous thing you've ever done?"

"Have you ever broken the law?"

"On a scale of 1–10, how funny would you say I am?"

"Do you like my new sweater?"

"Do you ever wish David Beckham was your dad?"

"Is that enough money, or do you need more?"

For the dad who has
EVERYTHING

Dads get the rough end of the stick when it comes to gifts. Socks, ties, screwdrivers, beer glasses, slippers and golf tees (when they don't play golf) are guaranteed to make any excited dad's heart sink. Help is at hand with our list of alternative gifts to make dads look forward to Christmas and birthdays again. (Dads – this is the page of the book you need to leave open in a location with a heavy footfall.)

DADTASTIC – WHY YOU'RE SO AWESOME

Instead of a screwdriver... buy a cocktail shaker
to mix a screwdriver.

Say "no" to slippers... and "yes" to a pedicure (or a manicure).

Banish beer... and bring on the wine-tasting experience.

A tie is a definite no-no... unless it's to wear
whilst spending restaurant vouchers.

Leave golf tees in the bunker... but afternoon tea
for two scores a hole-in-one.

Chutney will just get dad in a pickle... how about
an Indian takeaway instead?

Novelty socks amuse no one...
but cinema tickets to see a comedy will.

Car accessories... yes, an ice scraper might be useful at
Christmastime, but an ice maker is even better.

'World's Best Dad' paraphernalia... buy him something
swanky with a discreet designer label instead.

Anything (cushions, paperweights, jigsaws) personalized
with photos of children or grandchildren... should be
replaced by actually spending time with Dad.

Dad JOKES

Why do dads take an extra pair of socks when they go golfing?

In case they get a hole in one.

"Dad, did you get a haircut?"

"No, I got them all cut."

I told my wife she should embrace her mistakes.

She gave me a hug.

My friend was showing me his tool shed and pointed to a ladder.

"That's my stepladder," he said. "I never knew my real ladder."

79

I can't MULTITASK...

Movies, books, TV... sometimes the media delights in portraying what dads can't do. Let's rewrite the story and consider what they can do! (And they might not even realize it.)

But I can...

... be an incredible role model.

... show my family and colleagues that it's possible to have a good work-life balance.

... teach my children that hard work really does pay off.

... prove that you don't have to have good beginnings to create a happy, successful life.

... pass on everything my dad taught me.

... show my children that men do cry – and that that's okay.

... encourage my children to reach out to me when they need support.

... make mistakes and learn from them – no one said being a dad would be easy.

... smash stereotypes and do everything people think dads can't/shouldn't do.

... be there to provide the biggest hugs imaginable.

... share my failures so that my children can avoid the same ones.

... put my phone down when my family needs me.

... show the importance of kindness through acts, both small and large.

... share the things I love – films, songs, hobbies – so that my children understand a little about me.

... keep everyone I love safe.

... be honest, humble and fair – the things I would like my children to be too.

All about
YOU

"It's only when you grow up and step back from him –
or leave him for your own home – it's only then that you
can measure his greatness and fully appreciate it."

MARGARET TRUMAN

"Anyone who tells you fatherhood is the greatest thing
that can happen to you, they are understating it."

MIKE MYERS

"I believe that what we become depends on what our
fathers teach us at odd moments, when they aren't trying
to teach us. We are formed by little scraps of wisdom."

UMBERTO ECO

Bluff it:
GARDENING

Some dads have green fingers, but ALL dads can kill a plant. If gardening has become your 'dad job' (along with putting out the bins) and you're absolutely clueless, getting to grips with some of the basics should be enough to help grow a plant or two. Your garden doesn't have to be the envy of the neighbourhood, just alive.

1. Creating a great garden starts with inspiration. It doesn't need to be yours. Steal ideas from magazines and your neighbours' gardens.

2. Embrace nature. Some call it 'not bothering to garden', others call it 'rewilding'. Letting a portion of your garden return to a wild state is great for attracting wildlife and supports the environment.

3. Do your research! Don't pick plants just because they look pretty. Not all plants are easy to care for. Look for plants that are 'hardy' – this means they can tolerate low temperatures and being looked after by idiots. In short, make your garden as non-gardener friendly as possible.

4. Your garden can't be left to look after itself. Think of it like an extra child: it will need feeding, watering, hair cuts and talking to (if you're that way inclined). Provided you do all that, you will grow a healthy, well-rounded and mature garden. And, unlike kids, it won't answer back. Result.

5. You can't stick a plant anywhere. Lots of plants need full sunlight to thrive – so if you plant them in the shade, you're going to be sorely disappointed by the results. Figure out how much sunlight your garden gets and at what times. The best way to do this is with a garden chair and a bottle of beer.

6. Gardening can really stink. If your soil isn't great, it's a good idea to add more nutrients and oomph to it by digging in some compost. Yes, it will smell vile, but your plants will be the envy of your friends. If your nose can bear it, go a step further and add some delicious horse manure. Your NEIGHbours will love you (get it?).

7. Does the thought of mowing a lawn every weekend fill you with horror? Aside from the increased likelihood of having to make small talk with neighbours, maintaining a lawn can be a right royal pain in the behind. Do you really need the grass? (Your kids may argue "yes", but just remind them that there's a local park around the corner where they can kick a ball.) Consider the other options – decking, gravel, paving – that are less time-consuming to maintain than grass and provide a more even surface for standing your wine glass on.

8. 'Leggy' isn't always a good thing to be. Plants are leggy if they've grown too long and straggly. They do this because they're not getting enough light. Basically, they're stretching to try to reach a light source. It's a bit like when you wake up and are stretching to try to find your spectacles on your bedside table – although you're more likely to pull a muscle.

9. 'Dead heading' is not a thrash metal band's album title – it's a very important process in the garden. What it means is to remove dead flowers so that the plant can better use its energy to produce new flowers (rather than support dead ones). It's a bit like spring cleaning your friendship circle to get rid of the deadwood.

10. Slugs are your worst enemy. Yes, you can buy pellets to kill them and try all the old wives' tales BUT YOU WILL NEVER WIN. No matter how much copper wire you wrap around pots or how many crushed eggshells you sprinkle on the ground, you cannot faze a slug. (Actually, beer traps work quite well but what a waste of beer.)

The financial ADVISER

When dads sign up for the role of parent, few realize the extent of the skills they will need. Nose wiper, heart fixer and taxi driver – but none are so close to their wallet as the role of financial adviser.

"Dad, can I borrow some money?"

DAD SAYS:

"I'm not made of money, you know." *[The classic response.]*

"Can I borrow some of your time to mow the lawn in return?"

"Sorry, I'm having an out-of-money experience."

"Ah, money – I remember that from before I had kids."

"Dad, I really, really want to buy that!"

DAD SAYS:

"What's the hurry? It took me 10 years to save for one."

"Yes, but do you NEED it?"

"I really, really wanted to be a professional surfer.
Unfortunately, 'I want' doesn't always get."

"The Spice Girls really, really, really wanted to zigazig-ah.
The difference is, they had the money to do it."

"The best way to save money? Don't spend it!"

"Dad, I think it's time my weekly allowance went up."

DAD SAYS:

"I think it's time for your weekly chores list to get longer too, then."

"If you put together a needs analysis and a formal
presentation, I'll consider your proposal."

"When my salary goes up, I'll let you know."

"Theophrastus said: 'Time is the most valuable thing a man can spend.'"

What type of dad ARE YOU?

You're a dadtastic dad – otherwise why would your kids have bought you this book? But what type of dad are you? Or let's rephrase that: what type of dad do you think you are? (Be honest, you probably think you're way cooler than your kids do.) If you're brave enough, ask your kids to tell you what they think and see if you're on the same wavelength!

Sporty dad

Your life revolves around how your team are doing. The first thing you bought each newborn was a babygro in your team colours. When not watching sport from your armchair, you're out playing it and getting your kids involved too. Basically, no one in your family has ever had a lie-in at the weekend. Your sporty child adores you and your less sporty child will one day look back fondly at what you put them through.

Most likely to say: "Ssssh! I can't hear the game!"

Handy dad

You're up at the crack of dawn, pulling on your shorts and strapping on your tool belt. There are jobs to be done! Nothing gets thrown away in your house because you can pretty much fix anything. You've dug out a basement single-handedly and all your garden furniture is made from wooden pallets you brought home from work. If your kids want something, you make it for them!

Most likely to say: "I'll get my toolbox."

Busy dad

In true hunter-gatherer style, you work every hour of the day to keep your family fed and watered (and in the latest trainers). There have been occasions when your kids have forgotten who you are and have looked at you with confusion. You have zero weight when you tell your kids to get off their devices because you're the worst offender of all. At weekends, you and your kids like to go to the park – they'll play whilst you do a Zoom call.

Most likely to say: "Can it wait a minute?
I just have to take this call from Bob in Accounts."

Party dad

When your children arrived, life didn't change for you. If another dad bemoans their lack of a social life, you have no idea what they're talking about. You never fly solo when you're looking after the kids – as soon as you've put them to bed, your fellow party dads are at the front door clutching bottles and a pack of cards. Your favourite film is *The Hangover.*

Most likely to say: "Sleep is for children and for wimps."

Outdoorsy dad

Always found wearing a fleece, you're ready for a wild adventure (although your definition of 'wild' is very different to party dad's). You drive a vehicle that accommodates the family, dog, camping gear, paddleboards, kayaks, bikes and skis. Most of your family photos are taken on top of a hill and feature your children scowling and looking cold. If it were up to you, you'd be living off the land in a cabin in the woods with no wi-fi.

Most likely to say: "There's no such thing as bad weather, only bad clothes."

Funny dad

Jokes and pranks are the order of the day from the moment you wake up. Your family aren't sure whether to find you hilarious or irritating, but you're pretty sure you're the funniest person they know. A constant source of classic dad jokes, every time you tell the 'A horse walked into a bar...' joke you laugh as hard as the first time you heard it. That time you put carrot in the trifle has gone down in family history.

Most likely to say: "Pull my finger..."

Clever dad

You have filled your children with 'useful' information since the day they were born. School projects are your forte and you take the lead whenever bicarbonate of soda and a papier-mâché volcano are involved. Nothing delights you more than your kids asking you a question about the great unsolved mysteries of the universe. You're the go-to dad for quiz teams and will revise solidly for weeks in advance.

Most likely to say: "I'm no expert, but let me tell you what I think..."

Proud dad

Whether it's sports day, graduation or your child's first pee in the potty, your eyes always well up before anyone else's. You have a wallet full of well-thumbed photos (arranged chronologically) that you whip out to show complete strangers how proud you are of your kids. Your children's successes mean everything to you – and if you could rig up a neighbourhood tannoy to broadcast every little piece of news, you would.

Most likely to say: "Did I tell you about the time Johnny won the skipping race three years in a row?"

A dad's guide to TEXTING

Fed up with feeling excluded by the endless new text acronyms that your kids invent? Time to reclaim them for the dads!

....

ROFLBGY: Rolling on the floor laughing before grounding you

INMOM: I'm not made of money

NMN: No means no

DADTASTIC – WHY YOU'RE SO AWESOME

FOMD: Fear of missing dinner

HYTMCK: Have you taken my car keys?

RME: Resting my eyes

YNGOLT: You're not going out like that

IKIR: I know I'm right

FYI: Forgiving your ignorance

IAYF: I am your father

ILYB: I love you but...

ICYDHMSN: In case you didn't hear me say no

CTM: Call that music?

INDY: I'm not dead yet

YMSN: Your mum says no

TMA: Take my advice

BHABW: Banging head against brick wall

The last WORD

"A father is neither an anchor to hold us back nor a sail to take us there, but a guiding light whose love shows us the way."

Unknown